Vintage Recipes

Timeless and Memorable Old-Fashioned Recipes from Our Grandmothers

Louise Davidson

All rights reserved © 2019 by Louise Davidson and The cookbook Publisher. No part of this publication or the information in it may be quoted from or reproduced in any form by means such as printing, scanning, photocopying, or otherwise without prior written permission of the copyright holder.

This book is presented solely for motivational and informational purposes. The author and the publisher do not hold any responsibility for errors, omissions, or contrary interpretation of the subject matter herein. The recipes provided in this book are for informational purposes only and are not intended to provide dietary advice. A medical practitioner should be consulted before making any changes in diet. Additionally, recipes' cooking times may require adjustment depending on age and quality of appliances. Readers are strongly urged to take all precautions to ensure ingredients are fully cooked in order to avoid the dangers of foodborne illnesses. All the nutritional information contained in this book is provided for informational purposes only. This information is based on the specific brands, ingredients, and measurements used to make the recipe and therefore the nutritional information is an estimate, and in no way is intended to be a guarantee of the actual nutritional value of the recipe made in the reader's home. The author and the publisher will not be responsible for any damages resulting in your reliance on the nutritional information. The best method to obtain an accurate count of the nutritional value in the recipe is to calculate the information with your specific brands, ingredients, and measurements.

ISBN: 9781093133127

Printed in the United States

www.thecookbookpublisher.com

Contents

COOKING VINTAGE RECIPES — 1
BREAKFAST — 5
APPETIZERS — 15
POULTRY — 29
BEEF, PORK, LAMB, GAME — 45
FISH AND SEAFOOD — 65
VEGETARIAN AND SIDES — 75
SOUPS — 87
DESSERTS — 97
RECIPE INDEX — 131
ALSO BY LOUISE DAVIDSON — 133
APPENDIX — 135

COOKING VINTAGE RECIPES

It's twenty-five years since I had to say goodbye to my grandmother, but I think of her every day. I know my mother does, too, and always with a smile.

Times are changing, but those of us who are lucky will recall our grandmothers, or even our great-grandmothers. Raised in the teens and twenties, married in the thirties, and raising children during and after the second world war – this is a whole generation of women whose time was unique and shall never again come to pass. Raised by Victorian mothers themselves, they saw the days of women's suffrage, the lean years of the Great Depression, and the outbreak of two world wars. They did not enjoy many of the freedoms women have today, but their homes were so often clean and comfortable, their children were fed home-cooked meals, and they often took an active hand in the church and community around them.

My grandmother always had cookies, usually stored in a tin in the cupboard. Visitors were always welcome, and if they weren't quite expecting you for supper, well, they'd just put an extra potato in the pot. There was always enough to go around.

Photo albums are one way we can still connect with them, but there's another way we can do that. One way we can reach back through time and spend an hour together. Have you discovered it yet?

It's the recipe box.

Time travel by recipe card.

Nostalgia is a powerful thing, and many of us would love to explore the decades of the 1900s. In this book, we share with you some of the classics of each decade, from the 1920s through to the 1970s. Some will be foods you've heard of but might ever have tried, while others might be familiar to you already.

These foods would have been cooked on one of the old aga stoves, as pictured below. If you didn't have one as a child, they were large, enameled iron ovens with a stovetop, and the heat came from a wood-burning compartment inside (if you lived in a rural area), or by electricity, or gas, for those in a town or city. For the really old recipes, the temperature was usually measured by holding your hand out, so some will say only "medium" or "hot" oven. Also, people mention putting a pot on the back of the stove. There was usually less heat there and your pot wouldn't be in the way, so that's where the expression "put it on the back burner" came from. By the 1950s and 1960s, most kitchens would have had an electric range, a refrigerator, and a freezer.

These stoves, as you can imagine, served as a heat source as well, so you often found granny's rocking chair nearby, covered with a colorful homemade afghan.

Another big change that this time period saw was the advent of convenience foods. Between the 1940s and 1950s, improvements in refrigeration meant that frozen foods were plentiful, and they were cheap. More women were joining the workforce, and so frozen vegetables saved a lot of time. Also, the number of supermarkets in America doubled during this time, so the market for processed foods – both canned and frozen – was exploding.

These were prosperous times; people had money to spend. Companies took advantage of this by advertising their new processed foods as healthy and convenient, and women were happy to buy them.

Sadly, this also meant the end of an era. What used to take a number of people in the kitchen to accomplish was now managed by the mother alone. Now, there was less need for a rush of canning and preserving foods in the autumn. Recognizing that cooking and food preparation was becoming less satisfying for women, advertisers started to talk a lot more about entertaining. This put company back in the kitchen, at least to some extent.

But it was never quite the same. The multi-generational households are gone, for the most part. Children don't stand on chairs to wash dishes in the sink, and we don't have friends and sisters coming and going by the back door, chatting over a big bowl of peas to shell, peeling potatoes, or making pickles.

But if you look, you'll see a shift happening. We're realizing that the additives and extra salt and sugar in our processed foods aren't good for our families. We're noticing that we've become very dependent on factories and industry, and we'd like to be able to do more of these things ourselves – things like growing a garden, preserving our own foods, and cooking organic foods from scratch. And maybe, like me, women today are missing that feeling of sisterhood and finding it lonely in our modern kitchens.

I've been collecting the recipe boxes from the women in my own family: the handwritten cards and the magazine clippings, and once in a while I'll find a handwritten note or even a photograph. I love to handle those old cards ad follow the instructions the way they are written, because it makes me feel closer to the women I'm missing, and even some I never met.

I hope you enjoy them too!

Louise

BREAKFAST

German Pancakes

This American adaptation of German old-world pancakes may have come to be called "Dutch Babies" because of a mispronunciation of "Deutsch" (which means German). The began to appear in America in the early 1900s. They're made with simple and inexpensive ingredients, which might be why these timeless classics are still so popular today.

Serves 4 | Prep. time 10 min. | Cooking time 20 min.

Ingredients
2 tablespoons butter
3 large eggs
¾ cup whole milk
¾ cup all-purpose flour
1 tablespoon sugar
Pinch ground nutmeg
Confectioners' sugar, for dusting
4 lemon wedges
Syrup, optional
Fresh berries, optional

Directions
1. Preheat the oven to 425°F.
2. Melt the butter in a 10-inch ovenproof skillet (cast iron is best) inside the oven.
3. With a whisk, combine the eggs, milk, flour, sugar, and nutmeg until smooth. Pour the batter into the prepared skillet.
4. Bake at 425°F until puffy and golden, about 16–18 minutes. (The pancake will deflate as it cools.)
5. Dust with confectioners' sugar. Serve with your choice of lemon wedges, syrup, and berries.

Yankee Mush

This hot cereal is made with the most basic of ingredients, and yet it's so satisfying. We found a version of this recipe in Mrs. Wilson's Cook Book, published in 1920. It was a favorite of my grandfather's – he always had it with half a grapefruit and a single boiled egg.

Serves 4 | Prep. time 5 min. | Cooking time 30 min.

Ingredients
2 ½ cups water
¾ teaspoon salt
⅔ cup cornmeal

Optional toppings: cinnamon sugar, fruit preserves, brown sugar or honey, milk, dried fruit and nuts

Directions
1. In a medium saucepan, bring the water to a boil and add the salt.
2. Slowly and gradually add the cornmeal, stirring constantly to avoid lumps.
3. Reduce the heat to minimum and cook until the cereal has thickened, about 30 minutes.

Potato Pancakes

Potatoes were an important staple during the Depression because they were cheap and filling. This easy recipe can be made from leftovers and still has plenty of appeal today.

Serves 4 | Prep. time 10 min. | Cooking time 20 min.

Ingredients
2 cups mashed potatoes
1 egg
¼ cup all-purpose flour
2 tablespoons minced white onion or chives
1 teaspoon salt
½ teaspoon black pepper

¼ cup butter
Ketchup, sour cream, or syrup for serving

Directions
1. In a mixing bowl, combine the potatoes, egg, flour, onion or chives, salt, and pepper. Mix to combine.
2. In skillet over medium-high heat, melt 1 tablespoon of butter.
3. Scoop ⅓ cup of the potato mixture, form it into a patty, and place it in the butter. Working in batches and adding more butter as needed, continue until all the potatoes are used.
4. Serve with your choice of topping.

1950s Overnight Breakfast Bake

You might have thought that overnight casseroles were a new thing, but in fact they are not. After the war ended, people were glad to have bacon back, and we saw a lot more of that for breakfast! If you looked through some handwritten recipes from the time, you would likely see something like this. Remember when you're serving that what was considered a "portion" was a smaller amount at that time.

Serves 6 | Chill time 12 h. | Prep. time 10 min. | Cooking time 1 hour.

Ingredients

1 loaf of bread, crusts removed
6 eggs
3 cups milk
1 teaspoon dry mustard
1 teaspoon oregano
½ teaspoon black pepper
1 cup shredded cheese
1 ½ cups bacon, cooked and crumbled
¼ cup butter, melted
1 tablespoon fresh basil, chopped (optional)

Directions

1. Tear the bread into pieces and layer it in the bottom of a baking pan.
2. Beat the eggs and whisk in the milk. Add the mustard powder, oregano, black pepper, and cheese, and mix well.
3. Pour the custard mixture over the bread. Cover the baking pan, and place it in the refrigerator overnight.
4. In the morning, let the pan warm up on the counter while the oven preheats to 350°F. Uncover the dish and sprinkle on the bacon.
5. Pour the melted butter over the top, and bake for 1 hour, or until the egg is set in the middle.
6. Garnish with chopped fresh basil, if desired and serve.

Quiche

You might think that people were eating mostly home-cooked meals in the 1960s, but that's not the case. Processed foods were everywhere, and breakfast was no exception. Boxed cereals were very common, and many of them are the same ones we eat today, Shreddies, Honeycomb, Raisin Bran, and Corn Flakes!

Thankfully, in the 1970s we seem to have discovered quiche, and we really made a thing of it!

Serves 6–8 | Prep. time 10 min. | Cooking time 35 min.

Ingredients

6 slices bacon, cooked
1 9-inch pie shell (unbaked)
2 cups shredded cheese of your choice (8 ounces)
3 eggs, slightly beaten
1 ½ cups whole milk
½ teaspoon salt
½ teaspoon pepper
1 tablespoon butter, melted

Directions

1. Preheat the oven to 375°F.
2. Crumble the bacon evenly in the pie crust, and top it with the cheese.
3. Lightly beat the eggs with the milk, salt, and pepper, and pour over the bacon and cheese.
4. Drizzle the melted butter over the top of the quiche and bake for 35 minutes, or until the egg is set in the center.
5. Let it cool for 10–15 minutes before cutting.

APPETIZERS

Speakeasy Crab Dip

I found this recipe with my grandmother's books, printed in one of those little booklets. It's rich, and it's just the sort of thing they enjoyed in the roaring '20s.

Serves 8–10 | Prep. time 20 min. | Cooking time 15 min.

Ingredients

1 pound fresh mushrooms, medium-sized
8 ounces crab meat
¼ cup chives, minced
2 tablespoons pimiento peppers, minced
¼ teaspoon thyme
¼ teaspoon oregano
¼ teaspoon salt
¼ teaspoon black pepper
½ cup mayonnaise
¼ cup Parmesan cheese, grated
Paprika, to sprinkle

Directions

1. Heat the oven to 350°F.
2. Clean the mushrooms with a damp kitchen towel. Remove the stems and scoop out the gills.
3. Combine the crab, chives, pimientos, thyme, oregano, salt, pepper, and mayonnaise, and spoon the mixture into the mushroom caps.
4. Place the mushrooms in a shallow casserole dish and sprinkle with Parmesan and paprika.
5. Bake for 15 minutes. Serve warm.

Deviled Eggs

If we're talking about vintage appetizers, deviled eggs are where it's at! You'd find them on buffet tables dating back a few hundred years, but they really came to the forefront in the 1950s. If you think about it, have you ever been to a church social and not seen them on offer?

Serves 12 | Prep. time 15 min. | Cooking time 0

Ingredients
6 hard-boiled eggs
1 ½ tablespoons sweet relish
1 ½ tablespoons ketchup
2 tablespoons mayonnaise
½ teaspoon prepared mustard
Dash salt and pepper
Paprika, for garnish

Directions
1. Slice the eggs lengthwise and gather the yolks in a bowl. Mix in all the other ingredients but the paprika.
2. Stir to combine, and then spoon or pipe the yolk mixture back into the eggs. Sprinkle with paprika.
3. Refrigerate until ready to serve.

Chislic

A distinctive dish of South Dakota which locals are proud to serve as an appetizer is the delicious Chislic. It came to the state with the Germans settlers, and the family recipes have been passed down from the early 1800s. Grilled, seasoned and marinated cubes of meat deliver great flavor as a starter.

Serves 8-10 | Prep. time 10 min. | Cooking time 20 min.

Ingredients
2 pounds mixed meats of lamb, venison, and beef (or use only your favorite)
4 teaspoons Worcestershire sauce
1½ teaspoons salt
½ teaspoon freshly ground black pepper
1 teaspoon garlic powder

1 teaspoon onion powder
2 teaspoons chili powder
Oil for deep frying

Directions

1. Pat the meat with paper towels, trim any excess fat, and cut into bite-size cubes, no larger than ½ inch.
2. To a large bowl, add the cubed meat and the spices. Mix well, cover with plastic wrap, and place in the refrigerator to marinate for 2–3 hours.
3. Prepare short wooden skewers or toothpicks by soaking in cold water for 15–20 minutes.
4. Warm the oil of a deep fryer, or heat oil in a deep heavy bottomed saucepan on the stove over medium-high heat, to a temperature of 350°F.
5. While the oil is warming up, thread 5–6 cubes of meat onto each skewer.
6. When the oil is ready, working in batches, lower the meat skewers into the oil. Let them fry until browned and cooked through, about 2–3 minutes. Place the cooked meat on a plate lined with paper towels.
7. Serve with saltine crackers and a ranch dipping sauce, if desired.

Cucumber and Shrimp Canapes

Whether it's because of the time it takes or because we're all watching our carbs now, fancy little sandwiches have all but disappeared. What a shame! It only takes a few minutes to recreate that sense of having something special for a little snack, or as an appetizer.

Did you know that these tasty little sandwiches originated in France in the 1800s? Originally, they toasted little pieces of stale bread, and served them with savory toppings and drinks before dinner. Since the French make everything look so good, the British soon picked up the habit. In America, the trend really took off with the entertaining boom in the 1940s and 1950s.

Makes 48 | Prep. time 15 min. | Cooking time 0

Ingredients
For the sauce
1 cup mayonnaise

4 ounces cream cheese, softened
1 tablespoon minced onion
¼ teaspoon white vinegar
½ teaspoon Worcestershire sauce
½ teaspoon garlic powder
¼ teaspoon paprika
Pinch dried oregano
Pinch dried basil
Pinch dill weed

Other ingredients
12 slices bread: white, whole wheat, brown, or rye (or a combination)
2 medium cucumbers, peeled if desired, and thinly sliced
48 cooked shrimp
Additional dill weed, for garnish

Directions
1. The night before, combine the ingredients for the sauce. Cover tightly and refrigerate.
2. When you're ready to assemble the sandwiches, remove the crusts and cut the bread in 4. The bread should be only a little larger than the cucumber slice.
3. Spoon a little of the sauce onto the bread, and place a slice of cucumber on top, add shrimp. Garnish with a bit of dill weed, and enjoy!

Party Meatballs

In the 1960s, canned and processed foods were definitely a thing, and the party was starting. THIS is where the meatballs and grape jelly thing came from, in case you ever wondered! Here's your chance to give it a try.

Serves 12–15 | Prep. time 15 min. | Cooking time 30 min.

Ingredients
For the meatballs
2 pounds lean ground beef
1 cup bread crumbs

1 egg
¼ cup milk
1 teaspoon salt
½ teaspoon black pepper

For the sauce
1 (18-ounce) jar grape jelly
¾ cup chili sauce
1 (18-ounce) jar barbecue sauce
1 medium yellow onion, minced

Directions

1. Combine the ingredients for the meatballs until they are well mixed, but not overworked. Bake them on a cookie sheet at 375°F for 30 minutes (or until done.) Alternatively, you can fry them in a skillet and set them to drain on paper towel. These can be made ahead, if desired.
2. Combine the ingredients for the sauce.
3. When the meatballs are ready, pour the sauce over and gently stir to make sure they're all covered. You can heat them in a crock pot, or bake at 325°F until everything is heated through and the sauce is bubbly.
4. Serve with toothpicks for spearing.

Cheese Fondue

This party food was so popular in the late 1960s and early 1970s that it became a cliché.

Serves 10–12 | Prep. time 5 min. | Cooking time 20 min.

Ingredients

4 cups Swiss cheese, shredded (12 ounces)
1 cup Gruyère cheese, shredded (4 ounces)
2 teaspoons cornstarch
1 cup white wine
1 tablespoon lemon juice
⅛ teaspoon ground nutmeg
⅛ teaspoon ground black pepper

Things to dip:
cubed bread: rustic, hard rolls, or baguette
cooked meats: chicken, shrimp or ham
vegetables: cherry tomatoes, cooked mushrooms, cooked peppers, cooked potato

Directions

1. Combine the cheeses with the cornstarch, and set the bowl aside.
2. In a saucepan or double boiler, heat the wine and lemon juice until it steams. Add the cheese a little at a time, mixing constantly.
3. When everything is combined and hot, add the nutmeg and pepper.
4. Tip the sauce into a fondue pot and keep it warm. Best served right away with a choice of dippers.

Runza

Brought to Nebraska by German settlers in 1850s, runzas are meat-filled bread pockets made of seasoned ground beef, onion, garlic, sauerkraut, and cabbage wrapped with dough and baked to golden perfection. They make a delicious snack.

Serves 6–8 | Prep. time 30 min. | Cooking time 3–5 hours

Ingredients
2 tablespoons olive oil
1 medium onion, finely diced
1 garlic clove, minced
1 pound lean ground beef
1 cup of prepared sauerkraut, with the juices
½ small green cabbage, shredded
Salt and pepper

Frozen or fresh bread dough for 2 loafs, thawed if frozen
1 egg
4 tablespoons water
Melted butter (optional)

Directions
1. Place a cast iron Dutch oven or deep pan over medium heat and add the olive oil. Sauté the garlic and onion until fragrant and translucent, about 1–2 minutes.
2. Add the ground beef. Using a wooden spoon, break up any lumps and brown for 4–5 minutes, until it changes color. Season generously with salt and pepper. Drain the beef mixture to remove excess liquids.
3. Add the cabbage and sauerkraut. Stir a few times to combine the ingredients well. Cook on low heat for 2–2½ hours or until the filling has reduced and the cabbage becomes tender. (You can also use a slow cooker and cook on low for 3–4 hours.)
4. Preheat the oven to 400°F and line a baking sheet with parchment paper
5. Take the bread dough and roll it out to about ¼ inch thick. Cut into 4×8 inch rectangles.
6. In a small bowl, mix the egg with the water to make egg wash.
7. Spoon about ½ cup of the ground beef mixture into the center of each runza. Fold the dough pieces over and pinch to seal. Place on the baking sheet, seam side down. Brush the bread pockets lightly with the egg wash.
8. Bake the bread pockets for 20 minutes or until you see that the pastry has risen. Reduce heat to 350°F and bake for another 15–20 minutes until golden brown.
9. If desired, brush each runza lightly with some melted butter as soon as they are out of the oven. Allow to cool slightly before serving.

POULTRY

Chicken Fricassee

This recipe is similar to one found in *The International Jewish Cook Book*, which was published in 1919. My grandmother made it often.

Serves 4–6 | Prep. time 10 min. | Cooking time 1 hour.

Ingredients
1 whole chicken, about 5 pounds
1 small onion, chopped
1 parsnip root, peeled and chopped
1 carrot, peeled and chopped

1 stalk celery, chopped
1 teaspoon salt
1 teaspoon black pepper
1 teaspoon ground ginger
1 tablespoon flour
¼ cup parsley

Directions
1. Cut up the chicken into serving pieces.
2. Place a pot with a tight-fitting lid onto the stove, and put the chicken fat in the bottom of it.
3. Sprinkle the onion, parsnip, carrot, and celery on top of the chicken fat, and pour a few tablespoons of water over.
4. Season the chicken with the salt, pepper, and ginger, and layer the pieces on top of the fat with the largest ones on the bottom.
5. Cover the pot and place it on the back of the stove (over low heat) and add more water if necessary.
6. Cook for an hour. Toward the end, you can thicken the drippings with a little flour, and shake the pot a bit to prevent lumps.
7. When you're ready to serve, chop up some parsley and sprinkle it over the chicken.

Braised Duck with Mushrooms

This dish has been filling kitchens with its delectable scent for hundreds of years. Technically, it's *Duck aux Champignons*, a French dish that goes back at least to the 1800s. Because of the simple perfection of the ingredients, no modification can improve the flavor.

Serves 4–6 | Prep. time 20 min. | Cooking time 1 hour 15 min

Ingredients
2 wild ducks
2 tablespoons butter
1 large onion
2 cloves garlic
1 herb bouquet (sprigs of rosemary, thyme, sage, and parsley tied in a bundle)

½ can mushrooms
1 glass claret

Directions
1. Cut up the duck at the joints into serving pieces.
2. In a Dutch oven, melt the butter and brown the duck all over.
3. Add the onion, garlic, and herbs, together with a cup of water. Cover and simmer on low for an hour, until the duck is cooked through.
4. Add the mushrooms and claret and cook for 15 more minutes.
5. Let rest for 10-15 minutes before serving. Serve with mushrooms and sauce.

Chicken à la King

This recipe has been one of our family recipe favorites for years. It was a popular dish in the early 1900s and there are many stories about who created this recipe. The most credible is by George Greenwald, chef at New York's Brighten Beach Hotel, in the early 1900s. He prepared a special chicken dish one evening for the owners, Mr. & Mrs. E. Clark King II. Mr. King loved it so much that he asked for it to be on the menu right away and priced at $1.25! It became an instant success.

Serves 4 | Prep. Time 10 min. | Cooking time 30 min

Ingredients
1 tablespoon butter
1 tablespoon flour
Freshly ground pepper, to taste
¼ teaspoon salt
½ teaspoon paprika
1 tablespoon sherry
1 cup milk
½ cup cream
1 cup cooked chicken fillet, cut into cubes
¾ cup green peas
1 small carrot, diced
1 pimento, chopped
½ cup cooked mushrooms, cut into bite-size pieces (optional)
1 tablespoon green bell pepper, chopped (optional)
4 pre-baked puff pastry patty shells
Salt and pepper

Directions
1. Melt the butter in a saucepan over gentle heat, or in a double boiler.
2. Add the flour, pepper, salt, paprika, and sherry.
3. Gradually add the milk and cream, stirring constantly, until thickened.
4. Add the chicken, peas, carrots, pimento, mushrooms (optional) and bell pepper (optional) and cook 15 minutes longer or until thickened.
5. Serve in baked patty shells. Season with salt and pepper.

Chicken with Almonds

This is a chicken dish from wartime, the early 1940s. The chicken is simmered in a flavorful cream sauce and served over toast. It cooks up quickly, and though we don't use cloves and raisins in our entrées much anymore, they're very nice here.

Serves 4–6 | Prep. time 10 min. | Cooking time 30 min.

Ingredients
¼ cup butter, divided
2 tablespoons all-purpose flour
1 cup milk
1 teaspoon salt
¼ teaspoon black pepper
2 tablespoons minced onion
½ cup white wine
1 cup chicken stock
1 whole clove
½ bay leaf
3 cups diced, cooked chicken
¼ cup raisins

½ cup slivered almonds, minced
¼ cup sherry
3 egg yolks, lightly beaten
½ cup heavy cream
8 pieces hot toast, buttered

Directions
1. Melt half the butter in a saucepan and add the flour. Whisk until smooth, and stir in the milk. Season with salt and pepper, and bring it to a low boil. Cook it for a minute or two, then cover it and keep it warm.
2. In a large skillet, melt the remaining butter and brown the onion. Add the wine, stock, clove, bay leaf, and whisk in the white sauce. Cook for five minutes.
3. Remove the clove and bay leaf, and stir in the chicken, raisins, and almonds.
4. Just before serving, whisk together the sherry, egg yolks, and cream, and stir that in. Cook one minute, and then serve over hot toast.

Roast Goose

Thankfully, we don't have to pluck and clean our fowl anymore, because that was quite a process. These days we can enjoy a nice roast goose in fewer, simple steps. My grandparents often talked about the Christmas goose – this is how it was cooked.

*Serves 4–6 | Prep. time 30 min. |
Cooking time 1 hour 30 min.*

Ingredients
1 goose
3 cups mashed potato
¼ cup butter
6 onions, sliced
4 apples, peeled, cored, and sliced
12 sage leaves, chopped
Salt and pepper to taste

Potatoes, apples, carrots, for roasting

Directions
1. Preheat the oven to 350°F.
2. Rinse the goose and check to make sure it is fully plucked; remove any giblets stored inside.
3. In a skillet, melt the butter and add the onions, apples, and sage. Cook until they begin to soften.
4. Add the mashed potatoes and mix well. Season with salt and pepper.
5. Stuff the goose with the potato mixture, and place it on a trivet in a baking dish with a bit of water in the bottom, and some potatoes, apples, and carrots.
6. Bake for about an hour and a half (or until the internal temperature is 165°F).

Kentucky Hot Browns

This famous American open-faced sandwich was created in 1926 by chef Fred K. Schmidt in 1926 from the Brown Hotel in Louisville, Kentucky. It is a play on the of classic Welsh Rarebit cheese sandwich (for which you will find the recipe here). It was introduced for late dinners from the hotel as a different choice from the traditional ham and egg supper. This famous Southern recipe is sure to become your favorite, topped with roasted turkey and delicious Parmesan cheese. You will find yourself in food heaven! It's a great way to use turkey leftovers from Thanksgiving!

Serves 4 | Prep. time 10 min. | Cooking time 5 min.

Ingredients
4 thick white bread slices
12 ounces sliced roasted turkey
2 tomatoes, sliced
8 bacon slices, cooked
1 cup shredded Parmesan cheese
Mornay Sauce, warm (recipe follows)

Directions
1. Preheat broiler and place oven rack on the upper position at about 6 inches from heat source.
2. On a baking dish, place bread slices and broil until golden brown on each side, about 1 minute per side.
3. Arrange bread slices on 4 lightly greased individual baking dishes, and top with turkey slices.
4. Pour warm Mornay sauce over the turkey, and sprinkle each evenly with the Parmesan cheese.
5. Place under the broiler until the cheese is melted and golden, about 2-4 minutes.
6. Top with tomato slices and bacon, and serve.

Mornay Sauce

Yields approx.1 ½ cups

Ingredients
½ cup butter
⅓ cup all-purpose flour
1 ½ cups milk
¼ teaspoon salt
¼ teaspoon pepper
½ cup shredded Parmesan

Directions
1. Melt butter in a saucepan over medium- high heat.
2. Whisk in flour, and cook for 1 minute, whisking constantly.
3. Add milk and bring it to a boil. Reduce heat to medium-low, and continue cooking until it has thickened, about 3-4 minutes.
4. Whisk in Parmesan cheese, salt and pepper. Continue stirring until the cheese is melted. Serve immediately.

Chicken Paprika

Your family might still be using this recipe from the 1960s, but we'll include it here in case you haven't tried it. It's easy and delicious.

Serves 4 | Prep. time 10 min. | Cooking time 1 hour, 15 min.

Ingredients
2 tablespoons bacon grease
1 tablespoon butter
2 medium onions, chopped
1 ½ cups beef broth
1 tablespoon paprika
1 fryer chicken, cut into pieces
1 cup sour cream

Hot rice or pasta, for serving

Directions
1. In a deep skillet with a lid, heat the bacon grease and butter. Brown the onions and chicken. Add the broth and paprika. Bring it to a boil.
2. Reduce the heat to simmer. Cook for 1 hour, and serve over rice or pasta.

Baked Cornish Hen Cumberland

I found a clipping in my mother's recipe box from McCall's, 1973, for these Cornish hens. This recipe is adapted just slightly from that one.

Serves 4 | Prep. time 15 min. | Cooking time 1 hour 15 min.

Ingredients
4 (1-pound) Cornish hens
Salt and pepper to taste
¼ cup butter

For the sauce
3 tablespoons orange peel, shredded
2 tablespoons lemon peel, shredded
1 cup orange juice
1 cup currant jelly (apricot is also good)
½ cup Madeira (you can use any wine)
1 teaspoon dry mustard
½ teaspoon ground ginger
½ teaspoon salt

Directions
1. Preheat the oven to 500°F. Salt and pepper the inside of each hen and butter the outside. Arrange them breast up in a roasting pan.
2. Roast for 15 minutes, and then reduce the oven temperature to 400°F.
3. Turn the hens over and pour half a cup of water into the pan. Cover with foil and return to the oven for 30 minutes.
4. Meanwhile, make the sauce. In a medium saucepan, combine the peels with the orange juice. Bring it to a boil and simmer for 15 minutes. Add the other ingredients and simmer 20 minutes more.
5. Uncover the birds and turn them again to breast side up. Baste with the juices, and return them to the oven for 30 minutes, basting from time to time.
6. Serve the hens with a serving of sauce poured over.

BEEF, PORK, LAMB, GAME

Smothered Swiss Steak

Nothing beats coming in from outdoors on a cold winter afternoon to the smell of this dish bubbling away. This is our family recipe; I hope you like it. It's not from Switzerland; in fact, the name comes from the old way of tenderizing meat by hitting it with a mallet or rolling it with a rolling pin – "swissing."

Serves 4–6 | Prep. time 10 min. | Cooking time 1 hour 40 minutes.

Ingredients

2 pounds round steak, cut into serving pieces
½ teaspoon salt
½ teaspoon ground black pepper
¼ cup all-purpose flour
¼ cup shortening
1 onion, diced
1 stalk celery, diced
1 green bell pepper, thinly sliced
8 ounces mushrooms, sliced
2 cloves garlic, minced
¼ cup tomato paste
2 cups stewed tomatoes
2 cups beef broth
1 tablespoon Worcestershire sauce
1 tablespoon brown sugar
Mashed potatoes for serving

Directions

1. Preheat the oven to 325°F.
2. Using a meat mallet, pound the steaks on both sides.
3. Season the meat with the salt and pepper, and toss it in the flour to coat.
4. Melt the shortening in a Dutch oven and brown the meat.
5. On top of the meat, add the onion, celery, pepper, mushrooms, and garlic.
6. In a bowl, mix the tomato paste with the stewed tomatoes, beef broth, Worcestershire sauce, and sugar, and pour that over.
7. Cover, and bake for 1 ½ hours. Serve over mashed potatoes.

Cabbage Rolls

I was surprised to find that the cabbage rolls I detested as a child (the ones I love now and regularly inflict upon my own children) actually go back at least as far as the 1920s. I wonder if children then were a little more open minded.

These work well in your slow cooker, but your grandmother would have done them in the oven on low heat.

Serves 4–6 | Prep. time 20 min. |
Cooking time 4–5 hours (slow cooker) or 1 ½ hours (oven).

Ingredients
12 large cabbage leaves
1 ½ pounds lean ground beef
1 cup cooked rice

1 small onion, finely chopped
¼ cup milk
1 large egg, beaten
1 ½ teaspoons salt
½ teaspoon black pepper
1 cup tomato sauce
2 tablespoons brown sugar
1 tablespoon Worcestershire sauce

Directions
1. Boil the cabbage leaves until they are soft enough to work with (about 5 minutes).
2. In a bowl, mix the beef, rice, onion, milk, egg, salt, and pepper.
3. Scoop a portion of the meat filling into each cabbage leaf. Tuck in the sides, roll it up and pin it with a toothpick. Arrange the rolls in a baking dish.
4. Heat the oven to 325°F, if using.
5. Mix together the tomato sauce, brown sugar, and Worcestershire sauce. Pour this over the rolls.
6. Bake for 4–5 hours (slow cooker), or 1 ½ hours in the oven, until done.

Meat and Potato Patties

These kid-friendly patties, which I still love, have been around since the lean days of the Great Depression. It's still a great way to stretch a pound of meat.

Serves 4 | Prep. time 10 min. | Cooking time 25 min.

Ingredients
- 1 pound lean ground beef
- 1 cup potato, shredded
- 1 small onion, minced
- ¼ cup chives, chopped
- 1 large egg, beaten
- ½ teaspoon salt
- ¼ teaspoon black pepper
- 1 tablespoon butter

1 cup tomato juice
1 tablespoon all-purpose flour
¼ cup water

Directions
1. Mix together the beef, potato, onion, chives, egg, salt, and pepper. Form 4–5 patties.
2. Melt the butter in a skillet and brown the patties on both sides.
3. Pour in the tomato juice and cook until the patties are done in the middle.
4. Remove the patties from the pan.
5. Thicken the sauce with the flour and water, and serve it over top.

Sausage Stovies

Here's a no-fuss wartime supper your family will still enjoy. It hails from Scotland, where to "stove" something is to stew it. Therefore, variations of this meal always have potatoes, usually meat, and often onions as well. You can throw in whatever vegetables you like. We love mushrooms.

Serves 4–6 | Prep. time 10 min. | Cooking time 1 hour.

Ingredients
4 large potatoes, washed and sliced or diced
1 large onion, sliced
6 large sausages (or 12 links), casting removed and crumbled
1 teaspoon rubbed sage

½ teaspoon dried marjoram
½ teaspoon dried tarragon
1 ½ cups beef stock
Salt and pepper to taste

Directions
1. Butter a baking dish and place a layer of potato in the bottom. Layer on some onion and some sausage, and season with a sprinkle of the herbs.
2. Repeat the layers until all the ingredients are used, finishing with potato.
3. Pour the beef stock over the dish, and add salt and pepper to taste.
4. Bake in a medium oven (350°F) for 1 hour.

Shoulder Lamb Chops with Vegetables

I found this recipe card in my mother's box, from Betty Crocker in 1971. It has some of her preferences written on it – this is her version.

Serves 4 | Prep. time 10 min. | Cooking time 45 min.

Ingredients

4 shoulder lamb chops, 1 inch thick
¾ cup water
¼ cup soy sauce
2 beef bouillon cubes
2 cloves garlic, minced
1 medium onion, sliced
2 tablespoons cornstarch
¼ cup water
1 cup green beans
1 cup mushrooms, sliced
1 (8-ounce) can water chestnuts, drained and thinly sliced
1 green pepper, cut into thin strips
8 cherry tomatoes

Directions

1. Trim any excess fat from the chops and brown them in a skillet, draining as required.
2. Add the ¾ cup water, soy sauce, beef cubes, and garlic to the skillet, and bring the liquid to a boil.
3. Reduce the heat and add the onion. Cover and simmer for half an hour.
4. Remove the lid and transfer the meat to a platter.
5. Combine the cornstarch and ¼ cup water to make a slurry, and add this to the sauce in the pan. Stir and cook until it thickens, and then add the green beans, mushrooms, water chestnuts, green pepper, and tomatoes.
6. Arrange the chops back in the pan. Cover and cook 10 minutes.

Roast Venison

For most people who hunt these days, deer is usually what they're after. When I was little, father explained to me that hunting provided food for people, but it also kept the deer population from getting too big – this way, there would be more food for the ones who lived through the winter.

If there are any venison lovers in your family, they'll love this old family recipe. It's so simple, and the meat comes out lovely every time. If not, you can still make it with beef.

Serves 4–6 | Prep. time 10 min. | Cooking time 1 hour.

Ingredients

1 venison roast, about 2 ½ pounds
Soft Cottolene (this was a kind of shortening; you can use regular shortening)
Salt and pepper to taste
2–3 tablespoons flour
1 onion, sliced
1 carrot, sliced
1 small parsnip, sliced
1 potato, quartered
2 stalks of celery, cut in 1-inch pieces

Directions

1. Wipe the venison with a piece of damp cheesecloth and spread it with soft Cottolene. Sprinkle with salt and pepper.
2. Place the roast on a rack in a roasting pan, and sprinkle the meat and the pan with flour. Add the vegetables, and pour a little water over.
3. Bake in a hot oven (375°F) for an hour, basting every 10 minutes at first, then from time to time.

Barbecued Spareribs

This is my grandmother's recipe for pork spareribs, which she said came from the 1950s. What she referred to as "barbecue" we might call "sweet and sour," but either way, they're delicious and very tender.

Serves 4–6 | Prep. time 10 min. | Cooking time 90 min.

Ingredients

2 pounds spareribs
Salt and pepper to taste
1 tablespoon butter
1 small onion, finely chopped
½ cup water
½ cup ketchup
2 tablespoons brown sugar
1 tablespoon vinegar
1 tablespoon lemon juice
1 tablespoon Worcestershire sauce

Directions

1. Preheat the oven to 350°F.
2. Brown the ribs in batches in a Dutch oven.
3. In a separate bowl, combine all the other ingredients and pour the sauce over the ribs.
4. Cover, and bake for 90 minutes.

Boston Baked Beans

The origins of the Boston baked beans is very interesting. The native Americans were slow cooking beans in hot ashes hole in a clay pot long before we ever did. When the pilgrims from the Plymouth colony in the Boston area discovered the recipe in the 1620s. During the 18th century, when Boston was a large importer of rum from the Caribbean, they added molasses, residue from the distillation process, and salted pork.

This recipe has been in my family for generations. We use Maple syrup instead of brown sugar but either one can be used. Sweet and steaming hot, they never last long around our table. As the pilgrims, we still use clay beanpot to make this recipe but you still can make it in Dutch oven.

Serves 10–12 | Prep. Time 10 min. | Cooking time 1 hour 30 min

Ingredients

1 piece salted lard (or 6 strips of cooked and crumbled bacon)
1 pound dry navy beans, rinsed and soaked overnight
1 onion, diced finely
½ cup molasses
1 tablespoon dry mustard
½ cup packed brown sugar (or maple syrup)
Cold water
Salt and pepper to taste

Directions:

1. Preheat the oven to 300°F.
2. Add the beans to the clay pot. Add the onions, molasses, brown sugar, and mustard. Add cold water to cover the beans completely. Stir to combine the ingredient. Add the salted lard or bacon and press down so it's covered by the beans.
3. Bake for at least 4 hours, stirring every 30 minutes. Add more water, if needed.
4. The beans are done when sticky, thick, and tender.
5. Remove from the oven. Taste and season with salt and pepper to taste. Add brown sugar, if needed.

Liver and Onions

It was never my favorite thing to eat as a kid, but it's very high in vitamins A and B. It also has plenty of zinc and folate – but it's really high in cholesterol. My husband loves this old recipe, which is adapted a little from *The International Jewish Cookbook*, 1919.

Serves 4 | Prep. time 10 min. | Cooking time 1 hour.

Ingredients
2–3 tablespoons goose grease (or butter, or bacon fat)
1 large onion
4 slices calf's liver
2 tablespoons flour
½ teaspoon salt
1 bay leaf

5 whole cloves
2 peppercorns
Water, as needed

Directions
1. In a skillet with a good lid, melt the grease and cook up the onions.
2. Dredge the liver in the flour, and season with salt.
3. When the onions are soft, add the liver to the skillet. Put in the bay leaf, cloves, and peppercorns. Add a little water.
4. Cover, and let it cook on low for an hour, turning occasionally and adding more water if necessary.

Taylor Ham Sandwich

In northern New Jersey, this tasty and unique deli meat is called Taylor Ham, whereas in the south of the state, it's usually referred to as Pork Roll. It comes from Trenton, and has been served in New Jersey for more than 100 years. There are even two festivals devoted to it! If you don't live in New Jersey or neighboring states, you might have to order the ingredients online, but it's so worth it!

Serves 6 | Prep. Time 10 min. | Cooking time 10 min.

Ingredients

12 slices boxed Taylor Ham / Pork Roll
6 slices American cheese
6 Kaiser rolls
Lettuce, shredded
Russian or Thousand Island dressing
Cucumber, peeled and thinly sliced
Chips and/or cut vegetable sticks for serving

Directions

1. Make small incisions on each corner of each pork roll slice so it remains flat when it's fried.
2. Warm a large non-stick pan over medium heat. Add the pork roll slices and fry until golden brown, about 1–2 minutes per side. Work in batches so as not to overcrowd the pan.
3. Place a slice of cheese on 6 of the pork roll slices and cover the pan until the cheese is melted.
4. To assemble the sandwich, spread the bottom of the roll with Russian or Thousand Island dressing. Top with shredded lettuce and cucumber slices. Follow with the first pork roll slice (without the cheese). Top with the cheesed pork roll slice.
5. Close the roll and serve with a side of chips and/or vegetable sticks.

FISH AND SEAFOOD

Tuna Casserole

Canned tuna started to be available in the early part of the century, and by the 1950s we were seeing it regularly. Sometimes, as kids, we saw it on our plates, in the form of a tuna casserole. Home cooks at this time were in love with all the new "convenience" foods, and so the recipes often call for tinned soups. In the spirit of the times, this recipe does, too.

Serves 8 | Prep. time 15 min. | Cooking time 30 min.

Ingredients

8 ounces dried egg noodles
2 cups frozen peas
3 (5 ounce) cans tuna
2 cans condensed cream of mushroom soup
¼ cup minced onion
1 teaspoon garlic powder
1 cup milk
Salt and pepper to taste
4 cups corn flakes
⅓ cup butter, melted

Directions

1. Preheat the oven to 350°F and butter a casserole dish.
2. Cook the noodles according to the package directions. A minute or two before they're done, put in the peas so they can cook, too.
3. Meanwhile, drain the tuna and place it in a mixing bowl with the soup, onion, garlic powder, and milk. Mix well, and season to taste with salt and pepper.
4. Drain the pasta and peas, and gently mix them in with the tuna. Transfer the lot to the casserole dish and spread it out.
5. Crush the cornflakes and combine them with the melted butter. Sprinkle this over the top of the casserole.
6. Bake until it's hot and bubbly, about 30 minutes.

Baked Cod with Cream

The cod fishery was in trouble for a while, so it's nice to see the numbers climbing back to better levels. Some are still choosing not to eat it, but if you happen to pick some up, here's one way your great-grandmother might have cooked it. (Incidentally, you can use any white fish in this recipe.)

Serves 4–6 | Prep. Time 20 min. | Cooking time 15 min.

Ingredients

1 codfish (or 4–6 fillets)
Salt and pepper to taste
¼ cup butter
¼ cup flour
2 cups cream (heavy cream or 15%, or a mix)
½ cup bread crumbs
¼ cup minced parsley

Directions
1. Parboil the fish and remove the bones. Place the fish in a buttered casserole dish. Sprinkle with salt and pepper.
2. Melt the butter in a saucepan and mix in the flour until smooth. Cook a minute or two, and then gradually add 2 cups of cream. Cook to thicken, and pour the sauce over the fish. Sprinkle with bread crumbs.
3. Bake until the fish flakes easily with a fork, about 15 minutes.
4. Sprinkle with parsley, and serve.

Lobster Fricassee

Did you know that lobster used to be considered a waste product? In the early days of European settlers on the east coast of North America, they weren't quite sure what to do with the heaps and piles of these ugly crustaceans. They used them for bait and garden fertilizer, and the poor people ate them. They were fed to prisoners and servants, as well.

Then, in the 1880s, discerning diners in Boston and New York developed a taste for them – and the rest is history. Including this recipe, which came from the late 1800s.

Serves 4 | Prep. time 15 min. | Cooking time 15 min.

Ingredients

1 large lobster, boiled and shelled
1 cup chicken broth
½ cup cream
Salt and pepper to taste
½ teaspoon dried thyme
1 tablespoon lemon juice
2 tablespoons butter
Crackers, sour cream for serving

Directions

1. Cut the lobster into bite-sized chunks and place it in a saucepan with the chicken broth. Bring it to a boil, cover, and let it simmer a few minutes.
2. Add the cream and season with salt, pepper, and thyme. Let that heat up a bit. When it is steamy, add the lemon juice and butter.
3. Stir, and serve with crackers and or sour cream, if desired.

Kedgeree

When my mother was growing up, she didn't understand her parents' preoccupation with putting boiled eggs into things. I've tried this, though, and it's really quite nice. It's a British dish. Some say it's origins are in India, where it would have had lentils in it. British colonials brought it back to England, and from there it came to North America.

Serves 4 | Prep. time 5 min. | Cooking time 25 min.

Ingredients
1 pound haddock
½ cup dry rice
2 tablespoons butter
½ cup milk
2 teaspoons curry powder

1 teaspoon turmeric
3 tablespoons chopped parsley
3 hardboiled eggs, shelled and quartered

Salt and pepper to taste

Directions
1. Poach the fish until just done, and drain.
2. Boil the rice in lots of water with a bit of salt until it is almost cooked through. Drain.
3. Melt the butter in a skillet and add the rice and the fish, breaking it up a bit with the spoon. Pour in the milk and add curry powder and turmeric. Let it simmer until it is all absorbed.
4. Add the parsley, hardboiled eggs, and salt and pepper to taste, and serve.

Normandy Trout

When my grandmother's older brothers came home with trout from the creek, this was her mother's favorite way to prepare it.

Serves 4–6 | Prep. time 20 min. | Cooking time 15 min.

Ingredients
1–3 trout, depending on the size
Salt
1 onion, sliced
2 carrots, chopped
2 sprigs parsley
1 bay leaf
A few peppercorns
2 tablespoons butter
Yolks of 2 eggs
½ cup heavy cream
Pinch of cayenne

Directions
1. Clean the fish and sprinkle with salt and pepper. Place it in a pot with enough water to just cover. Bring it to a boil and reduce the heat to simmer.
2. After a few minutes, add the onions, carrot, parsley, bay leaf, peppercorns, and butter.
3. When the fish is cooked, remove it to a platter.
4. Mix the egg yolks with the cream and slowly add it to the cooking liquid. Cook to thicken, and season to taste with more salt and the cayenne pepper. Remove the bay leaf.
5. Serve the trout with the hot sauce.

VEGETARIAN AND SIDES

Creamed Peas on Toast

Another inexpensive meal from the Depression, this recipe is seldom seen today—but it's a tremendous comfort food for those who (like me) ate it growing up. Give it a try! It's really best on white bread, and put that margarine away. Use butter.

Serves 6 | Prep. time 5 min. | Cooking time 20 min.

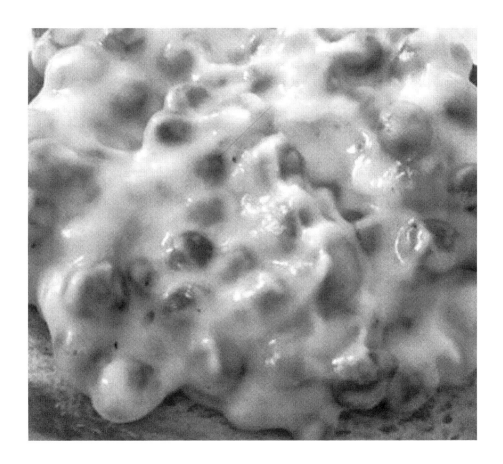

Ingredients

¼ cup butter
¼ cup all-purpose flour
1 ½ cups milk
1 teaspoon salt
2 cups frozen peas
10–12 slices hot buttered toast
Black pepper to taste

Directions

1. Melt the butter in a medium saucepan and stir in the flour to form a roux. Cook over medium-low heat for a minute or two, and then gradually whisk in the milk.
2. Season with salt, increase the heat to medium, and cook until the mixture thickens, about 5 minutes.
3. Add the frozen peas, and cook until heated through, thick, and steamy. (If it gets too thick, you can add a little more milk.)
4. Meanwhile, make and butter the toast.
5. Serve the toast with the peas on top, and season with black pepper to taste.

Creole Rice

There are so many recipes for this rice dish, but what's lovely about the old ones is the simplicity of the ingredients list. The 1920s cook used what was easily on hand.

Serves 4–6 | Prep. time 5 min. | Cooking time 20 min.

Ingredients

2 teaspoons butter or bacon grease
1 large onion, finely chopped
1 green pepper, finely chopped
1 cup canned tomatoes, rubbed through a sieve
3 cups cooked rice
2 teaspoons salt
1 teaspoon paprika
Optional: ½ cup ham or cooked sliced sausages

Directions
1. Melt the butter or bacon fat in a skillet and cook the onion and green pepper until softened.
2. Add the tomatoes, rice, salt, paprika, and meat if using, and cook to heat through.

Johnny Cake

This depression-era recipe makes good use of cornmeal, a common and inexpensive staple in America at that time – a variant of cornbread, really. There are dozens of recipes out there, but this is the one my great-grandmother used. You can bake it in one dish or make pancakes with it. It's gone by many names, one of which was "journey cake." This likely developed into "Johnny Cake."

Serves 8 | Prep. time 5 min. | Cooking time 30 min.

Ingredients

1 cup all-purpose flour
1 cup cornmeal
1 ½ teaspoons salt
1 teaspoon baking soda
2 eggs
1 cup buttermilk
¼ cup sugar (this can be omitted for serving with savory dishes)
¼ cup vegetable oil or bacon fat

Directions

1. Preheat the oven to 350°F and grease an 8-inch baking pan.
2. Combine the dry ingredients in a mixing bowl and whisk in the eggs, buttermilk, sugar, and oil.
3. Pour into the prepared pan and bake for 30 minutes, or until a toothpick inserted in the center comes out clean.

Curried Cabbage

Curry was the latest great thing in the 1940s, and cooks were trying it out in many different ways – some look better than others. We often make this dish even now; it's a nice way to switch up your sides.

Serves 6 | Prep. time 15 min. | Cooking time 30 min.

Ingredients

¼ cup butter
½ cabbage, thinly sliced
1 small onion, thinly sliced
1 tablespoon curry powder (or to taste)
1 teaspoon salt (or to taste)

Directions

1. Melt the butter in a pan or cast iron skillet over medium heat. Sauté the cabbage and onion until they are softened and begin to caramelize.
2. Sprinkle with curry powder and salt, and serve.

Welsh Rarebit

If you ask people today what "rarebit" is, I'm betting few can tell you – and that's a shame. We're talking about a vintage dish that was common all throughout the early 1900s, and our grandmothers almost certainly would have eaten it growing up. And since we're talking about cheese and toast here, I think it's time for this classic to make a comeback!

Serves 3–4 | Prep. time 15 min. | Cooking time 15 min.

Ingredients
2 tablespoons butter
2 tablespoons all-purpose flour
½ teaspoon mustard powder
½ cup whole milk

Dash Worcestershire sauce
2 cups grated cheese (your choice)
Salt and pepper to taste
6 slices bread of your choice

Directions
1. Melt the butter in a double broiler and whisk in the flour and mustard powder.
2. Gradually whisk in the milk and Worcestershire sauce and let it heat to a simmer, stirring frequently.
3. Stir in the cheese until melted. Season with salt and pepper. Allow the sauce to heat and thicken while you toast the bread.
4. Spoon the cheese sauce over the toast, and pop it under the broiler for a minute, or until cheese is golden as desired.

Colcannon

Here's a recipe for the ages. Colcannon – also known as "Bubble and Squeak" – is an old Irish dish that found its way onto many a table during World War II, at least according to the recipe in *Health for All Wartime Recipes*, 1942. You might recognize it from your grandmother's house; I know I do.

Serves 6 | Prep. time 10 min. | Cooking time 45 min.

Ingredients
5 large potatoes
2 leeks, chopped
¼ cup butter

2 cups curly kale
1 ¼ cups whole milk
2 spring onions, chopped
Salt and pepper to taste

Directions
1. Boil and mash the potatoes.
2. While the potatoes are cooking, melt the butter and cook the leeks and kale until wilted.
3. Add the greens to the potatoes together with the milk and spring onions. Season with salt and pepper to taste. Serve with butter, if desired.

SOUPS

Ham and Bean Soup

In the lean 1930s, everyone relied on beans and cured meats. This hearty soup is one way they were commonly combined.

Serves 10 | Soaking overnight | Prep. time 30 min. | Cooking time 1 h. 30 min.

Ingredients
3 cups navy beans (other beans can be used)
1 cup onion, diced
1 cup carrot, peeled and diced
½ cup diced celery

2 cups chicken broth
3 cups water
1 bay leaf
1 ham hock with meat (or 2 cups diced ham)
½ teaspoon black pepper
Parsley for garnish

Directions
1. Soak the beans overnight in a large bowl of water. Drain and rinse.
2. Place the beans in a Dutch oven, together with all the other ingredients. Bring it to a boil and simmer for an hour and fifteen minutes.
3. Remove the ham hock from the broth and cut off the meat in bite-sized pieces. Return the meat to the soup, and discard the bone. Remove the bay leaf.
4. Simmer for a few more minutes. If you want the soup to be a bit thicker, you can scoop out some of the beans and mash them, then return them to the pot.
5. Serve and garnish with parsley, if desired.

Vegetable Stew

For the first part of the 1940s, food was rationed because of the war. Meat, butter, sugar, and cheese were much harder to come by, even if you had the money. This meant that mothers had to come up with nutritious meals using what they had, and this flexible stew is a great way to use up vegetables that are a little past their peak.

Serves 6 | Prep. time 15 min. | Cooking time 30 min.

Ingredients
1 tablespoon butter
2 large onions, diced
2 cloves garlic, chopped
5–6 cups water
1 cube chicken or vegetable bouillon

4 medium potatoes, peeled and chopped
4 carrots, peeled and sliced
½ white cabbage, sliced
½ cauliflower, chopped
1 (28-ounce) can tomatoes, diced
1–2 cups additional vegetables (peas, green beans, corn, etc.)
Salt, pepper, and herbs to taste

Directions
1. Melt the butter in a soup pot and cook the onions until they are softened. Add the garlic and cook until fragrant.
2. Add the water and flavoring cube and bring the soup to a low boil. Add the potatoes and carrots, and simmer for 5 minutes.
3. Add the remaining vegetables and seasonings, and simmer for 15 more minutes, until the vegetables are fork tender.

Amish Church Soup

This is another simple and nutritious soup that deserves more attention these days. It hails from the Depression, and still makes a great lunch. My mother ate it with biscuits, but I like a nice crunchy artisan loaf.

Serves 6 | Prep. time 5 min. | Cooking time 30 min.

Ingredients
¼ cup butter
3 cups cooked navy beans
1 small carrot, finely diced
4 cups milk
4 slices buttered bread, cut into small chunks
Salt and pepper to taste
2 tablespoons fresh chives, chopped

Directions
1. Melt the butter in a Dutch oven and brown the onions.
2. Add the beans, carrot, and milk, and bring it up to a boil, add the bread and let simmer for 5-10 minutes, and then take it off the heat.
3. For thicker soup. Mash some of the beans and stir them back in.
4. Season with salt and pepper, stir-in the chives, and serve.

New England Clam Chowder

When food is scarce or rationed, those who live by the sea can sometimes augment their diet with a few dozen clams, freshly dug by the children. You can enjoy the same seaside simplicity today – clams have not changed at all. (My grandmother also ate periwinkles, but we're not suggesting you go that far.)

Serves 8 | Prep. time 20 min. | Cooking time 1 hour.

Ingredients
6 medium potatoes, peeled and chopped
3 cups water
1 large onion, sliced
1 small carrot, shredded
1 ½ quarts whole milk
¼ cup butter

2–3 dozen clams
Parsley, chopped
¼ cup heavy cream
Salt and pepper to taste
Soup crackers for serving

Directions
1. Place the potatoes in the pot with the water and bring them to a boil. Simmer 10 minutes, or until they are about half cooked.
2. Add the onion, carrot, milk, and butter, and bring it almost to a boil over medium heat, stirring often. Cook about 15 minutes, until the onion and potato are tender
3. Add the clams with their juices and the parsley. Reduce the heat to medium-low and cook 20 minutes, until the clams are cooked and the broth is nicely flavored. Stir in the cream, and season with salt and pepper to taste.
4. Serve with crackers, if desired.

Partridge Soup

Partridge was commonly eaten from hundreds of years ago right up until the mid-twentieth century. It was in season from September through the early winter months, but it wasn't always the most tender of meats. I found this recipe in my aunt's box, but I don't recall eating it myself. She says they sometimes used wild turkey, instead.

Serves 8 | Prep. time 15 min. | Cooking time 2 hours.

Ingredients
2 partridges
2 tablespoons butter
2 medium onions, shredded
3 stalks celery
1 large carrot

1 small turnip
3 medium potatoes, chopped
1 teaspoon sugar
Salt and pepper to taste
2 quarts water or stock
Shopped fresh herbs for garnish such as chives, parsley, thyme, or rosemary

Directions
1. Cut the partridges into pieces and fry them in the butter until they are browned and quite tender.
2. Remove the breasts, legs, and wings, and leave the rest of the bones and cuttings to flavor the broth. Add the onions and celery and cook a few minutes.
3. Add the water or stock, and simmer an hour.
4. Strain the broth, discarding the bones and vegetables. Add the broth back to the pot with the carrot, turnip, potatoes, sugar, and the partridge meat.
5. Bring it to the boil and reduce to a low simmer. Cook 30 minutes. Skim the broth, and season with salt and pepper to taste.
6. Garnish with favorite fresh herbs and serve.

DESSERTS

Pineapple Upside-Down Cake

Hawaiian pineapple became a hit in America in the 1920s because it was easy to ship in cans, and ladies' magazines of the day loved to feature recipes for ways to use it. Couple this delicious fruit with a traditional sponge cake and a cast iron skillet, and you've got the classic we still love today.

Serves 8 | Prep. time 15 min. | Cooking time 45 min.

Ingredients

2 cups all-purpose flour
2 teaspoons baking powder
½ teaspoon salt
2 large eggs, separated
½ cup butter, softened
1 cup granulated sugar
½ cup whole milk
1 ½ teaspoons vanilla extract

For the topping
3 tablespoons butter
1 cup paced brown sugar
6–8 pineapple rings, canned
6–8 maraschino cherries (more if desired)

Directions

1. Preheat the oven to 350°F.
2. Prepare the topping in a 10-inch cast iron skillet by melting the butter and sugar together over medium heat. When the sugar is dissolved, arrange the pineapple rings in the caramel and place a cherry inside each*. (Add more if you like.) Set the skillet aside.
3. Sift together the flour, baking powder, and salt, and set them aside.
4. In a clean bowl, beat the egg whites until they are light and frothy.
5. In a separate bowl, beat the sugar with the butter until it is fluffy. Add the egg yolks, and mix them in.
6. Add the milk in increments, alternating with the dry ingredients.
7. Fold in the vanilla and egg whites.

8. Spoon the batter over the pineapple and bake for 45 minutes, or until a toothpick inserted in the center comes out clean.
9. Loosen the edges with a knife, and carefully flip the cake onto a serving plate.
10. If you haven't added the cherries, do so now.
11. Cool, and serve!

*Some people prefer to add the cherries after the cake is baked.

Kuchen

North Dakota serves an authentic recipe that originated with German settlers from the 1850s and has been passed down for generations. Kuchen is an amazingly comforting sweet dough cake, which is filled with fruit and custard. My mom makes hers with pears instead of apples, when in season.

Serves 6–8 | Prep. time 1 hour. | Cooking time 20 min

Ingredients
Kuchen base (2 pies)
2 large eggs
1½ cups sugar
1 teaspoon salt
2 cups warm milk
1 (1¼-ounce) package rapid rise yeast

6 cups all-purpose flour
½ cup oil
Vegetable oil for greasing

Fruit custard filling
4 cups heavy cream
6 eggs
1 cup sugar
Dash salt
4 apples, peeled, cored and sliced
2 teaspoons cinnamon
2 tablespoons sugar

Directions
1. To prepare the kuchen pie crusts, whisk the eggs, sugar and salt in a large bowl. Slowly add the warm milk and then mix in the flour and yeast.
2. Grease a clean large bowl generously with vegetable oil. Transfer the dough to this bowl, cover with plastic wrap, and set aside in a warm area so it can rise. It should double in size.
3. Preheat the oven to 350°F and grease a 9-inch baking pan.
4. To make the custard, add the eggs, sugar, heavy cream and salt to a heavy-bottomed saucepan. Whisk over medium heat until the custard thickens. Remove from heat.
5. Prepare the pie crust by lightly dusting a surface with flour and rolling out half the dough into a thick, round circle to fit in a 9-inch deep pie plate. Grease the pie plate with cooking spray. Place the dough in the pie plate. Repeat for the second pie.

6. Arrange the apple slices evenly on top of the dough of each pie.
7. Mix the cinnamon with 2 tablespoons of sugar. Sprinkle evenly over the apples. Pour half of the custard into each kuchen.
8. Place the kuchen in the oven and bake for 20 minutes. Remove from the oven and let cool down for at least 30 minutes before placing in the refrigerator until you are ready to serve.

Holiday Cake

This is a traditional recipe for a lovely, simple cake, courtesy of the English. It's very good with a hot cup of tea. In the early 1900s and before, it was common to sweeten baked goods with raisins and currants.

Serves 12 | Prep. time 15 min. | Cooking time 2 hours

Ingredients

3 ½ cups all-purpose flour, sifted
2 teaspoons baking powder
1 teaspoon salt
1 cup chopped almonds
1 cup raisins
¼ cup lemon peel, cut fine
1 cup butter or other shortening
2 cups sugar
1 ½ cups shredded coconut
2 teaspoons vanilla
1 teaspoon almond extract
10 egg whites, stiffly beaten

Directions

1. Preheat the oven to 250°F and grease an angel food pan. Line the bottom with paper.
2. Sift the flour with the baking powder and salt, then sift again three times to combine. Sprinkle ½ cup over the fruits and mix well.
3. Cream the butter with the sugar and mix well. Add the remaining flour a little at a time.
4. Add the coconut, floured fruits, vanilla, and almond extract. Fold in the egg whites.
5. Transfer the batter to the pan and bake for 2 hours.

1920s Rice Pudding

Oh, the wholesome simplicity of this pudding just makes my heart swell. I like it warm but chill yours if you prefer that. I was taught to make something like this when the oven is on anyway, such as when you're roasting a turkey.

Serves 4 | Prep. time 15 min. | Cooking time 3 hours

Ingredients
5 tablespoons long grain rice (dry)
1 quart whole milk
½ cup cane syrup
½ teaspoon salt
½ teaspoon ground cinnamon
Pinch ground nutmeg
½ cup raisins

Directions
1. Grease a casserole dish.
2. Combine all the ingredients and pour them into the dish.
3. Cook on the stovetop at low heat for 3 hours, stirring often.

Strawberry Chiffon Pie

The difference between a chiffon pie and a cream pie is that the chiffon uses gelatin and meringue in the filling rather than only cream. Traditional recipes – these pies go back to the 1920s – might have you beat fresh egg whites, but this one uses meringue powder - a safer bet if you're concerned about salmonella bacteria.

Serves 6-8 | Chill time 4 hours | Prep. time 25 min. | Cooking time 10 min.

Ingredients
For the crust
18 graham crackers, crushed
⅓ cup butter, melted
¼ cup sugar

For the pie filling
1 pint fresh strawberries
½ cup sugar
1 tablespoon unflavored gelatin
¼ cup cold water
½ cup very hot water
1 tablespoon lemon juice
Pinch salt
1 cup whipped cream
1 ½ tablespoons meringue powder
¼ cup water
¼ cup sugar, divided

Directions
1. Preheat the oven to 375°F.
2. Crush the graham crackers and stir in the melted butter and sugar. Press the mixture into 9-inch pie plate to form the crust.
3. Bake for 10 minutes, and then set it aside to cool.
4. Meanwhile, crush the strawberries and stir in the sugar. Set aside for 30 minutes.
5. In a clean bowl, pour the cold water over the gelatin to soften it, and then add the hot water to dissolve it.
6. Add the lemon juice and salt to the strawberries. Stir in the dissolved gelatin.
7. Chill for about an hour, until the berry mixture begins to hold its shape a little when you move it with a spoon.
8. Fold the whipped cream into the berry mixture.
9. Beat the meringue powder with the water and half the sugar until soft peaks form. Slowly add the rest of the sugar and continue beating just until stiff peaks form.
10. Fold the meringue mixture into the strawberry mixture, and spread it in the prepared crust. Refrigerate until firm.
11. Top with additional whipped cream, if desired.

Snickerdoodles

These cookies might be familiar to you, but it places them in a different light to realize that people have been eating them for over a hundred years. They likely originated in New England.

Serves 6-8 | Prep. time 25 min. | Cooking time 10 min.

Ingredients

1 ½ cups sugar
½ cup butter
½ cup shortening
2 eggs
1 teaspoon vanilla
2 ¾ cups all-purpose flour
1 ½ teaspoons cream of tartar
1 teaspoon baking soda
½ teaspoon salt

Cinnamon sugar

2 tablespoons sugar

2–3 teaspoons cinnamon

Directions

1. Preheat the oven to 400°F.
2. In a large mixing bowl, beat the sugar, butter, and shortening until light and fluffy.
3. Add the eggs and vanilla, and mix well.
4. Add the flour, cream of tartar, baking soda, and salt, and stir until the dough is uniform.
5. Make the cinnamon sugar. Take scoops of the cookie dough, roll them in balls, and roll the balls in the dough.
6. Bake on cookie sheets for 8–10 minutes, just until set. Transfer to a rack right away, and cool.

Plum Charlotte

I love this recipe for using up stale bread and fruit that might be past its peak. This was common in the 1940s, when people were very careful not to let anything go to waste. Feel free to substitute whatever fruit and bread you have.

Serves 4 | Prep. time 15 min. | Cooking time 45 min

Ingredients
8 slices white bread, torn or made into crumbs
1 pound plums, sliced (you can add in an apple, peach, or berries if you prefer)
½ cup sugar
1 teaspoon orange zest
¼ cup butter
1 cup orange juice

Directions
1. Butter a baking dish, and set the oven to 375°F.
2. Put a layer of bread in the bottom of the baking dish, and cover with a layer of fruit, a sprinkle of sugar, a bit of orange zest, and a few dots of butter.
3. Repeat the layers until the ingredients are all used, finishing with bread and butter.
4. Pour the orange juice over, and bake for 45 minutes, or until the edges are bubbly and the top is golden.

Chocolate Chip Oat Cookies

Here's one for the ages! It seems some things haven't changed much – this recipe goes all the way back to the 1930s, where it appeared on a cereal box. (Raisins optional, cranberries are good too.) If you have little ones, this recipe is nice to use because they're not too sweet.

Serves 12 | Prep. time 15 min. | Cooking time 10 min

Ingredients
1 cup packed brown sugar
2 large eggs
½ cup whole milk
¾ cup vegetable oil
1 teaspoon vanilla extract
2 cups all-purpose flour

1 teaspoon baking soda
1 teaspoon salt
1 teaspoon ground cinnamon
1 teaspoon ground nutmeg
2 cups old-fashioned oats
½ cup semisweet chocolate chips
½ cup raisins

Directions
1. In a large mixing bowl, combine the sugar, eggs, milk, oil, and vanilla.
2. Sift in the flour, baking soda, salt, cinnamon, and nutmeg. Mix well.
3. Add the oats, chocolate chips, and raisins, and let it sit for 10–15 minutes.
4. Heat the oven to 350°F.
5. Drop the batter by the spoonful onto ungreased baking sheets, and bake for 10 minutes, or until golden around the edges.

Jelly Roll

This was my absolute favorite when I was a little girl, and my kids love it too. It's the simplest recipe on a small bit of paper, but it works every time.

Serves 6 | Prep. time 15 min. | Cooking time 15 min

Ingredients
For the cake
3 eggs
1 cup water
2 teaspoons baking powder
1 cup sugar
1 cup flour
1 teaspoon vanilla
Pinch salt
¾ cup jam of your choice

For dusting
¼ cup icing sugar

Directions
1. Preheat the oven to 350°F and grease a 9x11 baking sheet.
2. Combine the ingredients and mix well. Spread them in the pan.
3. Bake 15 minutes, or until golden and cooked through.
4. Spread with jam and roll immediately. Dust with icing sugar.

Divinity

This is a candy I'd only read about in books, so I was delighted to come across a recipe for it in *the Neighborhood Cook Book* when we were cleaning out a cupboard. This recipe is from 1914.

Serves 12 | Prep. time 10 min. | Cooking time 15 min

Ingredients
3 cups sugar
1 cup corn syrup
¾ cup water
3 egg whites
2 cups chopped walnuts or pecans
1 tablespoon vanilla

Directions
1. Line a baking sheet with parchment paper.
2. Place the egg whites in a bowl and beat with an electric mixer until stiff peaks form and set aside.
3. Combine the sugar, corn syrup and water in a large saucepan and cook over medium-high heat.

4. Stir constantly while cooking until the liquid reaches approximately 260°F on a candy thermometer. If you do not have a candy thermometer, a drop of the mixture put into a glass of icy cold water will form a ball and hold its shape.
5. Remove the saucepan from the heat and slowly start to drizzle the syrup into the egg whites while beating on high.
6. Add the vanilla and continue beating on high until the candy takes on a glossy appearance.
7. Quickly stir in the nuts and drop by rounded spoonfuls onto the baking sheet.
8. Set aside and allow to cool and harden slightly before serving.

Old-Fashioned Plum Pudding

We used to have this every Christmas, but it's been years since I've seen it. I was glad to find this handwritten recipe of my aunt's, because I would like to continue the tradition. We made it in cans and cut thick slices to steam over boiling water and serve with hard sauce.

NOTE! She writes that it's a very old recipe, and you use a coffee cup to measure these things, not a teacup. (I think this is probably close to a measuring cup, and not the large mugs we use today.) I just love the imprecision of it. Women who made this probably learned it from their mothers, going by habit, instinct, memory, and observation.

Serves 4 | Prep. time 30 min. | Cooking time 4 hours | 1 month to ripen

Ingredients

1 cup suet
1 cup bread crumbs
½ pound citron
3 cups flour
1 teaspoon baking soda
1 teaspoon baking powder
2 teaspoons cinnamon
½ teaspoon ground ginger
½ teaspoon ground cloves
½ teaspoon salt, or to taste
1 pound currants
2 pounds raisins
½ cup chopped walnuts
4 eggs, lightly beaten
1 cup dark brown sugar
1 cup molasses
1 cup milk
1 cup apple jelly

Hard sauce
2 tablespoons butter
2 tablespoons flour
½ cup brown sugar
1 cup boiling water
½ teaspoon salt
1 teaspoon vanilla
2 tablespoons rum, or to taste

Directions

1. Grind the suet, bread, and citron through a meat grinder (or pulse a few times in a food processor).
2. In a separate bowl, combine the flour, baking soda, baking powder, spices, and salt.
3. Separately, combine the currants, raisins, and walnuts. Take one cup of the flour mixture and dredge the fruit with it.
4. Beat together the eggs, brown sugar, molasses, milk, and apple jelly, and then fold everything together until combined.
5. Ladle the batter into molds or cans, and steam for 4 hours.
6. The pudding keeps well and is best if you let it sit a month. Serve with hard sauce.
7. To make the hard sauce, melt the butter in a medium saucepan, and whisk in the flour until smooth. Cook for a minute or so.
8. Mix in the brown sugar and boiling water, and cook over medium heat until it thickens to your liking.
9. Stir in the salt, vanilla, and rum.

Angel Pie

Angel pie dates back to the 1930s and the recipe has been passed down to the next generation. The pudding flavor can differ from cook to cook. My grandmother used to make it with lemons. And this is her recipe. If you like meringue, this will definitively be a hit in your family. You need to plan ahead for this pie as the filling should be refrigerated at least 8 hours before serving.

Serves 8 | Chill time 8 hours | Prep. time 15 min. | Cooking time 8 min.

Ingredients

For the meringue pie crust
Butter and flour for greasing and dusting
3 extra large egg whites
1 pinch cream of tartar
1 teaspoon pure vanilla extract
¾ cup white sugar

For the lemon filling
5 egg yolks
½ cup sugar
¼ cup lemon juice
Zest of 1 lemon
1 cup

Whipped Cream Topping
1 cup heavy cream, chilled
2-4 tablespoons confectioner's sugar
1 teaspoon vanilla
Gelatin to stabilize cream (optional)
¼ tablespoon water

Directions

For the meringue pie crust
1. Pre-heat the oven to 275°F and place oven rack in the middle position.
2. Coat a 10-inch deep pie pan with butter and lightly flour the pan. A glass pie pan such as Pyrex works best. Remove excess flour by reversing the pan over the sink.
3. In an electric stand mixer with the whisk attachment on, add the egg whites, vanilla, and a pinch of tartar. Beat on low speed until foamy.
4. Increase speed to high and gradually add the sugar. Beat until stiff peaks form.
5. Spread the meringue evenly into the pie dish with a spatula or the back of a wooden spoon.

6. Place into the oven and bake for 1 hour. Turn off the oven and let the meringue shell rest in the oven for 1 more hour. Make sure not to open the oven door as the meringue continues to dry up.
7. Remove from the oven and let cool completely.

For the lemon filling
8. While the pie shell is cooling down, prepare the filling.
9. Beat the yolks until they are thickened, and heat them gently in a double boiler.
10. While continuously beating, add the sugar, lemon juice, and zest.
11. Continue cooking and stirring until the filling is lightly colored and thick.
12. Remove the mixture from the heat and let it cool completely.
13. Add the lemon filling to the meringue pie crust, cover with plastic wrap, and refrigerate for at least 8 hours and up to 12 hours.

For the topping
14. If you are using gelatin, heat the water and add the gelatin, stirring until it is completely dissolved.
15. Let the gelatin cool down a little, but don't let it set.
16. Whip the cream to soft peaks, and gradually add the sugar and vanilla while whipping.
17. Add the gelatin in a thin stream while whipping continuously.

To assemble
18. Take 1 cup of the whipped cream topping and gently fold it into the lemon filling.
19. Fill the meringue crust with the rest of the filling.
20. Spoon the remaining whipped cream topping over the filling, and chill.

Banana Cream Pie

When the summer comes and the antique cars take to the roads again, I sometimes think about the lifestyle those people are remembering – the 1950s, and the days of sock hops and diners. This recipe hails from then, and it's just the sort of thing you might order in one of those classic diners.

Serves 6 | Chill time 6 hours | Prep. time 10 min. | Cooking time 30 min.

Ingredients
For the crust
1 ¼ cups all-purpose flour
¾ teaspoon salt
1 tablespoon sugar
½ cup butter, cold
2–4 tablespoons ice water

For the filling
1 cup sugar
⅓ cup cornstarch
1 teaspoon salt
3 cups whole milk
4 egg yolks, beaten
3 tablespoons butter
1 teaspoon vanilla extract
2–3 bananas, sliced

Topping
2–3 cups whipped cream, for topping

Directions
1. Make the crust. Preheat the oven to 375°F.
2. In a mixing bowl, combine the flour, salt, and sugar. Cut in the butter until none of the lumps are larger than a pea.
3. Add the ice water a tablespoon at a time, mixing lightly with a fork, until the pastry is moist enough to cling together when pressed into a ball.
4. Roll out the dough, and arrange it in a 9-inch pie plate. Trim and flute the edges, and pierce the bottom with a fork.
5. Bake 10–12 minutes, or until the crust is golden brown. Set it aside to cool
6. In a saucepan, prepare the filling. Mix the sugar, cornstarch, salt, and milk. Cook until it bubbles, stirring constantly.
7. Beat the egg yolks, and then stir in a small amount of the hot filling, whisking constantly, to temper the egg. Add a bit more and mix until smooth, and then add this back to the pot.
8. Bring the pot to a slow boil, and stir for two minutes.
9. Add the butter and vanilla, and refrigerate for 30 minutes.
10. Spoon half the pudding into the cooled crust, and cover with banana slices. Add the rest of the pudding, cover, and refrigerate until set, at least 6 hours.
11. Serve topped with whipped cream.

Flapper Pie

Another wonderful recipe that has been lost in time. My grandmother on my father's side used to make it often for her family. It was on all the menus in dinners restaurant in the 1920s. This recipe was written on a piece of paper that I found in an old cookbook my grandma gave when I got married. I have made it a few times and it always impresses.

Serves 6-8 | Prep. time 20 min. | Cooking time 10-15 min

Ingredients

Graham Cracker Crust
1 ¼ cups graham cracker, finely crushed
¼ cup melted butter
½ cup sugar
Dash cinnamon

For the filling
2 ½ cups milk
½ cup white sugar
¼ cup cornstarch
3 egg yolks
1 teaspoon vanilla
Pinch salt
Meringue topping

Directions

To make the crust
1. Mix the ingredients thoroughly. Set aside 2 tablespoons for garnish.
2. Press the mixture into a pie pan to form a shell, and refrigerate to set.

To make the filling
3. In a saucepan, combine the filling ingredients and cook over medium heat, stirring constantly.
4. Continue cooking until the custard has thickened.
5. Allow the mixture to cool while preparing the meringue topping.

To assemble and bake
6. Preheat the oven to 350°F.
7. Spread the filling in the crust while it is still slightly warm, and spoon the meringue on top.
8. Swirl the meringue with a fork and swirl to form peaks.
9. Bake until the meringue is golden brown (about 10-15 minutes). Sprinkle with the reserved crust mixture to garnish.

Jefferson Davis Pie

Created in the honor of President Jefferson during the civil war era, this pie is decadent and a close cousin to the chess pie consisting of a brown sugar custard with dates, raisins, and pecans. It's delicious and won't stay for long. I found this recipe in my aunt's recipe box and have done regularly over the years.

Serves 6-8 | Prep. time 10 min. | Cooking time 55 min.

Ingredients

½ cup golden raisins
½ cup chopped dates
½ cup pecans
3 tablespoons flour
1 teaspoon cinnamon
¼ teaspoon allspice
Pinch ground nutmeg
½ teaspoon salt
1 cup light brown sugar
1 stick unsalted butter, softened
1 cup light brown sugar
5 large egg yolks
1 ½ cups heavy cream
Blind baked 9-inch plain pastry shell
Whipped cream, for garnish

Directions

1. Preheat the oven to 325°F.
2. Place the raisins, dates, and pecans in a food processor or blender and run it until the mixture is finely ground. Spread this over the bottom of the pie shell.
3. Mix the flour, cinnamon, allspice, nutmeg, and salt together. Set it aside.
4. Cream the butter and brown sugar in a mixer. Add the yolks one at a time, mixing until well blended.
5. Add the flour mixture and cream alternately, stirring to combine.
6. Pour the filling into the pie shell.
7. Bake until the filling has thickened but is not too firm (about 55 minutes).
8. Serve chilled, topped with whipped cream.

RECIPE INDEX

BREAKFAST _____ 5
  German Pancakes _____ 5
  Yankee Mush _____ 7
  Potato Pancakes _____ 9
  1950s Overnight Breakfast Bake _____ 11
  Quiche _____ 13
APPETIZERS _____ 15
  Speakeasy Crab Dip _____ 15
  Deviled Eggs _____ 17
  Chislic _____ 19
  Cucumber and Shrimp Canapes _____ 21
  Party Meatballs _____ 23
  Cheese Fondue _____ 25
  Runza _____ 27
POULTRY _____ 29
  Chicken Fricassee _____ 29
  Braised Duck with Mushrooms _____ 31
  Chicken à la King _____ 33
  Chicken with Almonds _____ 35
  Roast Goose _____ 37
  Kentucky Hot Browns _____ 39
  Mornay Sauce _____ 40
  Chicken Paprika _____ 41
  Baked Cornish Hen Cumberland _____ 43
BEEF, PORK, LAMB, GAME _____ 45
  Smothered Swiss Steak _____ 45
  Cabbage Rolls _____ 47
  Meat and Potato Patties _____ 49
  Sausage Stovies _____ 51
  Shoulder Lamb Chops with Vegetables _____ 53
  Roast Venison _____ 55
  Barbecued Spareribs _____ 57
  Boston Baked Beans _____ 59
  Liver and Onions _____ 61

Taylor Ham Sandwich ___ 63
FISH AND SEAFOOD ___ 65
   Tuna Casserole ___ 65
   Baked Cod with Cream ___ 67
   Lobster Fricassee ___ 69
   Kedgeree ___ 71
   Normandy Trout ___ 73
VEGETARIAN AND SIDES ___ 75
   Creamed Peas on Toast ___ 75
   Creole Rice ___ 77
   Johnny Cake ___ 79
   Curried Cabbage ___ 81
   Welsh Rarebit ___ 83
   Colcannon ___ 85
SOUPS ___ 87
   Ham and Bean Soup ___ 87
   Vegetable Stew ___ 89
   Amish Church Soup ___ 91
   New England Clam Chowder ___ 93
   Partridge Soup ___ 95
DESSERTS ___ 97
   Pineapple Upside-Down Cake ___ 97
   Kuchen ___ 100
   Holiday Cake ___ 103
   1920s Rice Pudding ___ 105
   Strawberry Chiffon Pie ___ 107
   Snickerdoodles ___ 109
   Plum Charlotte ___ 111
   Chocolate Chip Oat Cookies ___ 113
   Jelly Roll ___ 115
   Divinity ___ 117
   Old-Fashioned Plum Pudding ___ 119
   Angel Pie ___ 122
   Banana Cream Pie ___ 125
   Flapper Pie ___ 127
   Jefferson Davis Pie ___ 129

ALSO BY LOUISE DAVIDSON

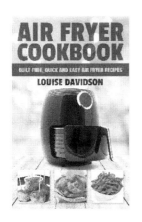  

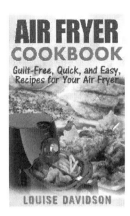
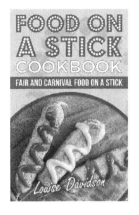
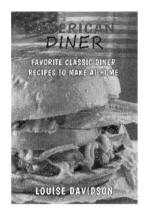

APPENDIX

Cooking Conversion Charts

1. Measuring Equivalent Chart

Type	Imperial	Imperial	Metric
Weight	1 dry ounce		28g
	1 pound	16 dry ounces	0.45 kg
Volume	1 teaspoon		5 ml
	1 dessert spoon	2 teaspoons	10 ml
	1 tablespoon	3 teaspoons	15 ml
	1 Australian tablespoon	4 teaspoons	20 ml
	1 fluid ounce	2 tablespoons	30 ml
	1 cup	16 tablespoons	240 ml
	1 cup	8 fluid ounces	240 ml
	1 pint	2 cups	470 ml
	1 quart	2 pints	0.95 l
	1 gallon	4 quarts	3.8 l
Length	1 inch		2.54 cm

* Numbers are rounded to the closest equivalent

2. Oven Temperature Equivalent Chart

Fahrenheit (°F)	Celsius (°C)	Gas Mark
220	100	
225	110	1/4
250	120	1/2
275	140	1
300	150	2
325	160	3
350	180	4
375	190	5
400	200	6
425	220	7
450	230	8
475	250	9
500	260	

* Celsius (°C) = T (°F)-32] * 5/9
** Fahrenheit (°F) = T (°C) * 9/5 + 32
*** Numbers are rounded to the closest equivalent

Image Credits

Introduction
Image source: https://www.pinterest.ca/pin/477944579179190324/

German Pancakes
By Andrawaag - Own work, CC BY-SA 4.0,
https://commons.wikimedia.org/w/index.php?curid=73819503

Chislic
By Gomboc2008 via Wikimedia Commons
https://commons.wikimedia.org/wiki/File:Kegchislicsmall.jpg

Chicken Paprika
By Kobako - photo taken by Kobako, CC BY-SA 2.5,
https://commons.wikimedia.org/w/index.php?curid=777368

Kentucky Hot Brown Sandwich
By Shadle - Own work, CC BY-SA 3.0,
https://commons.wikimedia.org/w/index.php?curid=4136793

Taylor Ham Sandwich
By Tomwsulcer - Own work, CC0,
https://commons.wikimedia.org/w/index.php?curid=19973256

Tuna Casserole
Free download image from Pixabay

Jefferson Davis Pie
By Drmies - CC BY-SA 3.0, https://en.wikipedia.org/w/index.php?curid=48510510

Made in the USA
Las Vegas, NV
04 November 2020